T0341979

Introduction:
What is Macramé? 2

Getting Started 4

Projects 8

>>>>>>>>> Getting Started >>>>>>>>>

Before you start work on a project, take some time to familiarize yourself with a few common techniques you will encounter throughout this book. These include basic knots and methods for splicing cords and wrapping cords neatly.

Basic Knots

These simple knots will be used throughout the book to start or finish projects and to join two colors of cord together.

Lark's Head Knot

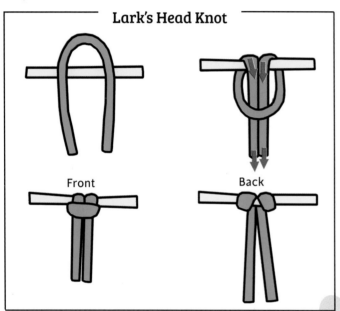

Front

Back

Overhand Knot

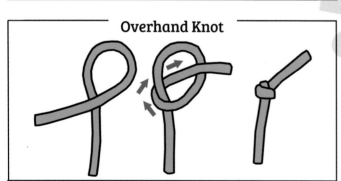

Square Knot

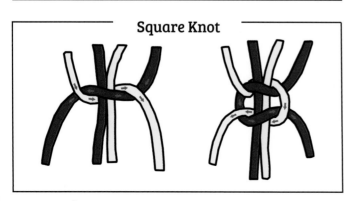

Reef Knot

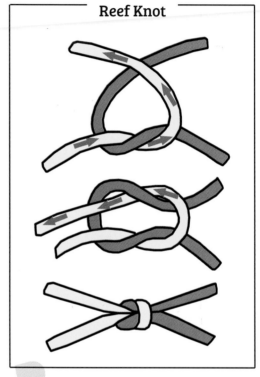

About Metric

Throughout this book, you'll notice that every measurement is accompanied by a metric equivalent. Inches and feet are rounded off to the nearest half or whole centimeter unless precision is necessary (note that some larger measurements are rounded off to the nearest meter). Please be aware that while this book will show 1 yard = 100 centimeters, the actual conversion is 1 yard = 90 centimeters, a difference of about 3 15/16 (10cm). Using these conversions, you will always have a little bit of extra cord if measuring using the metric system.

Hello! Macrame

Totally Cute Designs for Home Décor and More

SAMANTHA GRENIER

Design
Originals

an Imprint of Fox Chapel Publishing

www.d-originals.com

Introduction:

What is Macramé?

Macramé is the art of tying knots in cord or similar materials to create decorative items. It has a long history, likely originating with Arabic weavers, and has experienced popularity around the world at countless times in history. Both the United States and Europe experienced a macramé craze in the 1960s and 1970s as it grew to be a popular craft. The most prevalent macramé items, found in most homes, were the plant hanger and the macramé owl, but other projects like lampshades, jewelry, clothes, and wall hangings were also popular. At the height of the trend, *Vogue* magazine produced a book on macramé, bringing it into the world of high fashion.

With all the different types of cord available on the market today, macramé is again becoming popular as an incredibly versatile craft. Knot tying can be done with hundreds of different materials, from embroidery floss, ribbon, and yarn to hemp, cotton rope, and braided craft cord. Furthermore, the range of macramé projects is virtually endless. Thin embroidery floss can be combined with decorative knotting techniques to create delicate jewelry pieces, while thick rope can be combined with traditional marine knots to create functional items. This book takes advantage of sturdy craft cord to make home décor and other items that will withstand everyday wear and tear.

Whether you're looking for your next home décor project or want a new fashion piece to add to your wardrobe, macramé is sure to get you what you want. Pick a project and get started!

Acquisition editor: Peg Couch
Copy editors: Sue Kern, Laura Taylor
Cover and layout designer:
Ashley Millhouse
Editor: Katie Weeber
Photographer: Scott Kriner

ISBN 978-1-57421-868-8

© 2014 by Pepperell Braiding Company and New Design Originals Corporation, *www.d-originals.com*, an imprint of Fox Chapel Publishing, 800-457-9112, 1970 Broad Street, East Petersburg, PA 17520.

Printed in the United States of America
First printing

Infinity Bundles

Bundling long lengths of cord (3 yd. [300cm] or longer) together is a great way to stay organized and keep the cord from tangling. Use this quick and easy method to form an infinity bundle, which will keep your cord tangle free and accessible at all times.

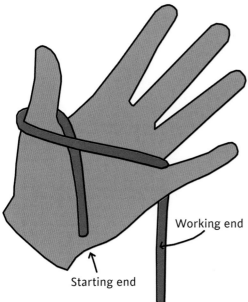

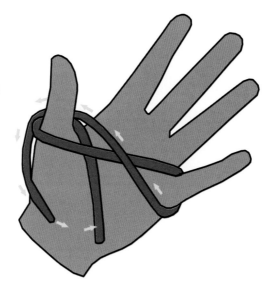

1| Loop one end of the cord around your thumb on top of your palm. Bring the rest of the cord across your palm and pass it between your ring finger and pinky.

2| Bring the working end of the cord around your pinky, across your palm, and around your thumb, forming a figure eight.

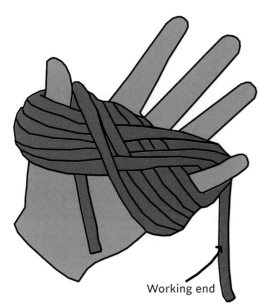

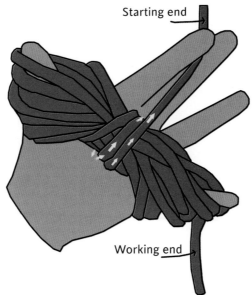

3| Continue wrapping the cord around your pinky and thumb in a figure eight pattern until the working end measures 12"–24" (30.5–61cm).

4| Wrap the starting end of the cord around the middle of the bundle to hold it in place. Tuck the loose end into the wrap. When you are ready to use the cord, gently pull on the working end to release some cord from the bundle.

Recommended Materials

Macramé can be done with any number of materials, from embroidery floss, to rope, to ribbon, to yarn. Most of the projects in this book were made with sturdy braided craft cord in varying thicknesses. The author used Bonnie and Amy cord, which can be found at your local craft store. Enjoy exploring all of the different ways you can use craft cord in your macramé projects.

Splicing

Splicing allows you to join two pieces of cord together practically seamlessly. This means you can add length to a cord if you are running short, or you can splice two colors together. Use the method below with hollow cord, 4mm thick or thicker.

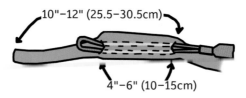

1| Feed the splicing tool into the hollow center of the first cord by passing the tool between the woven strands that form the cord, about 10"–12" (25.5–30.5cm) from the end. Feed the tool through the center of the cord, and bring it out 4"–6" (10–15cm) from the entry point.

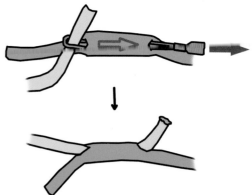

2| Bring the end of the second cord through the splicing tool, and use the tool to pull the second cord through the center of the first cord.

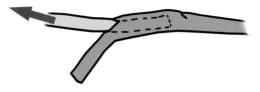

3| Gently tug on the second cord, pulling the end into the center of the first cord.

4| Repeat steps 2–3 to bring the end of the first cord through the second cord.

5| Tug the two cords in opposite directions to bring the end of the first cord into the second cord. If necessary, trim any excess cord coming out of the entry points.

Wrapping

This wrapping technique is used to hold multiple lengths of cord together securely and neatly on projects ending with many lengths of cord that cannot easily be finished with a simple knot. Wrapping is commonly used to begin or end plant hangers.

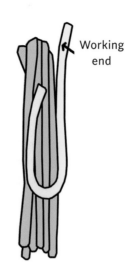

Working end

1| Bundle the cords to be wrapped together. Using one end of the wrapping cord, form a loop on top of the bundle.

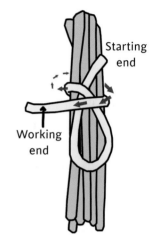

Starting end

Working end

2| Bring the working end of the wrapping cord around the bundle, making the wrap as tight as possible. Make sure the starting end of the wrapping cord extends above this first wrap.

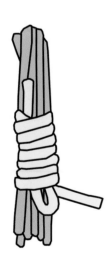

3| Continue tightly wrapping the cord bundle until only a small portion of the original loop extends beyond the bottom of the wrap.

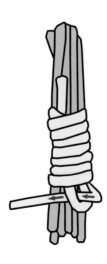

4| Pass the working end of the wrapping cord through the bottom loop.

5| Gently pull on the starting end of the wrapping cord to bring the bottom of the loop and the working end up into the wrap.

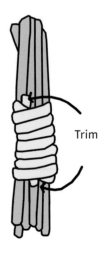

Trim

6| Trim both ends of the cord even with the edges of the wrap.

Projects

Making your own home décor projects and bags means you can customize each one to fit your personal taste and style by working in the colors and materials of your choice. Try getting started with simpler projects, like the Hanging Candleholders (page 28) and the Retro Plant Hangers (page 31). Then try your hand at making a bag or a rug. For a really ambitious project that is sure to impress friends and family, try the hanging chair (page 40) or hammock (page 45). These pieces are true showstoppers that will demonstrate all you've learned about macramé.

Market Tote >>> »»»» »»»»» » »» » »»»»» »

FINISHED SIZE: 12" x 12" (30.5 x 30.5cm) with 10" (25.5cm) handles

This sturdy little tote is perfect for picking up produce and other yummy goodies at your local market.

TOOLS & MATERIALS

- 4mm craft cord
    - Thirty-eight 3 yd. (3m) lengths for purse body
    - One 1 yd. (1m) length for guideline
    - Four 3½ yd. (3.5m) lengths for handles
    - Two 4 yd. (4m) lengths for handles
- Grill lighter
- Scissors

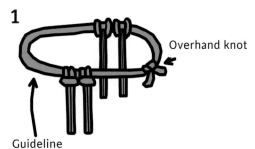

1| Form the 1 yd. (100cm) guideline cord into a loop that is 12"–16" (30.5 x 40.5cm) in diameter. Tie the ends of the cord together in an overhand knot to hold the loop in place. This is the mouth of the bag.

2| Find the center points of two of the 3½ yd. (350cm) cords and attach them to the guideline loop using lark's head knots, positioning the knots next to each other. Repeat with the remaining 3½ yd. (350cm) cords, positioning them directly opposite the first two cords attached to the guideline (figure 1). These cords form the center strands of the handles.

3| Center one 4 yd. (400cm) length of cord behind a set of handle center strands attached to the guideline. Tie a square knot around the center strands with the 4 yd. (400cm) cord (figures 2–3). Continue tying square knots around the center strands until the handle is 10"–12" (25.5–30.5cm) long, or until the two working strands are about 3" (7.5cm) long. Tuck the ends of the working strands into the underside of the handle, trim, and melt the tips. Repeat to form the second handle.

4| Position the loose end of a handle against the guideline to form the handle into a loop. Make sure the handle is not twisted. Tie each of the four center strands of the handle to the guideline using a double half hitch (figure 4). Do not trim these strands; they will be knotted into the body of the bag. Repeat for the second handle.

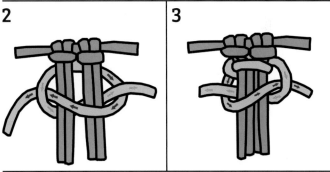

Tie strap ends to guideline using double half hitches

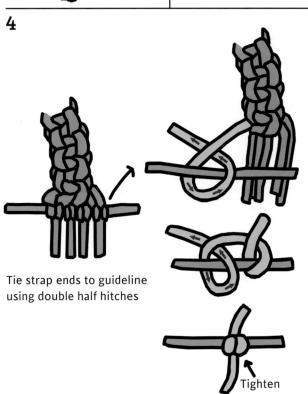

Tighten

Macramé

5| Tie all of the 3 yd. (300cm) cords onto the guideline using lark's head knots. Evenly distribute the cords around the guideline.

6| Divide the mounted working strands (including the handle center strands from step 4) into twenty-eight groups. There will be three strands in each group. Use the three strands from one group to tie seven half knots to form a spiral (figures 5–7). Repeat with the remaining groups.

7| Take two spirals that are side by side. Use two strands from the left spiral and one strand from the right spiral to tie seven half knots (figures 8–9). Repeat with all the remaining strands until the row is complete. This alternates the spirals in the first row with those in the second row.

8| Repeat step 7 (figures 8–9) to form alternating rows of spirals. Tie nine to ten rows, until the bag is about 12" (30.5cm) long.

9| To form the bottom of the bag, turn it inside out and press it flat with your hands. Pair off the cords, making sure each cord on the front of the bag has a partner opposite it on the back of the bag. Starting at one side of the bag, tie the front and back cord pairs together using double twist square knots (figures 10–12). Repeat across the bottom of the bag until all pairs are tied together.

10| Trim all cord ends to about ¼" (0.5cm) long, and melt the tips with a grill lighter to prevent fraying. Turn the bag right side out.

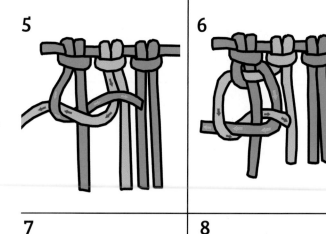

5

6

7

8

9

Row 2

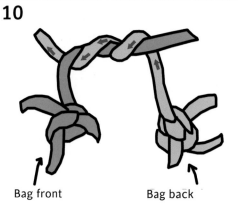

10

Bag front   Bag back

11

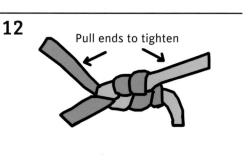

12

Pull ends to tighten

Messenger Bag/Laptop Case »»»»»

FINISHED SIZE: 16" x 12" x 1¼" (40.5 x 30.5 x 3cm) with 1 yd. (100cm) strap

This sophisticated design works for everyone from students to professionals. If you're feeling extra crafty, add a lining with pockets to hold even more!

TOOLS & MATERIALS

- 4mm craft cord:

  One 3 yd. (300cm) length in royal blue

  Twenty 7 yd. (700cm) lengths in navy

  Eleven 4 yd. (400cm) lengths in royal blue

  Two 11 yd. (11m) lengths in navy

  One 14 yd. (14m) length in royal

  One extra 8"–10" (20.5–25.5cm) length in navy

- Project board (or sheet of foam core)

- 10–15 T-pins

- 6"–8" (15–20.5cm) of ¾" (2cm) hook-and-loop tape

- Sewing needle

- Coordinating thread

- Scissors

- Grill lighter

1| Center and pin the 3 yd. (300cm) cord horizontally along one long edge of the project board. This is the guideline. Using lark's head knots, tie the 7 yd. (700cm) and 4 yd. (400cm) cords to the guideline in the following pattern: one royal blue, two navy. End with a royal blue cord. Position the attached strands so they span 16" (40.5cm) along the guideline (figure 1).

2| Starting from the left side, take the first four navy strands and weave them together as shown in figure 2. Starting with the top strand, tie the two right navy strands onto the adjacent royal blue strand using a double half hitch for the right side (figure 3). Repeat with the two left navy strands, tying them using a double half hitch for the left side (figure 4). The end result will look like figure 5.

1

2

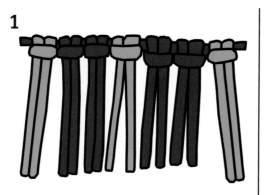

Weave center strands together

3   Double half hitch (right side)

Adjust and tighten

4   Double half hitch (left side)

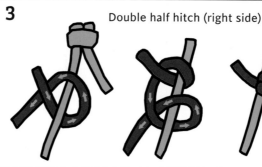

Adjust and tighten

5

Hello!

6

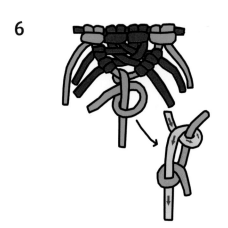

3| Tie the two center royal blue strands together using alternating half hitches (figure 6).

4| Repeat steps 2 and 3 with the remaining strands. To finish the edges, take the first four strands on the left side and tie the top navy strand to the outer royal blue strand using a double half hitch. Adjust the navy strand so the end points in toward the center of the design (figure 7). Then tie the navy strand to the inner royal blue strand. Repeat with the second navy strand, tying it to the outer royal blue strand and then to the inner royal blue strand. Tie the two royal blue strands at the outer left edge together with alternating half hitches. The end result will look like figure 8. Repeat with the first four strands on the right side.

5| Continue the weaving and knotting pattern until the bag is 30" (76cm) long (figure 9). Shift and repin the project to the board as needed as you work to achieve the desired length. To finish, trim and weave the ends of the working strands into the underside of the bag. Leave the guideline strands free. Melt any exposed working strand ends to prevent fraying. Remove the bag from the project board.

6| Take the short extra cord piece and mount it on the project board. Use lark's head knots to tie the two 11 yd. (11m) cords and the 14 yd. (14m) cord to it, positioning the royal blue cord between the two navy cords. Adjust the cord lengths as shown in figure 10.

7

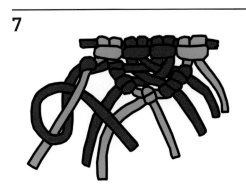

8

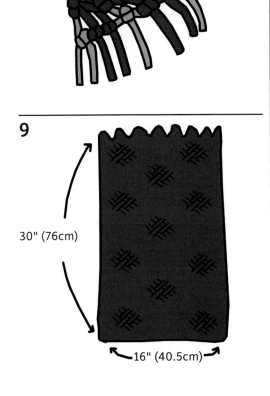

9

30" (76cm)

16" (40.5cm)

10

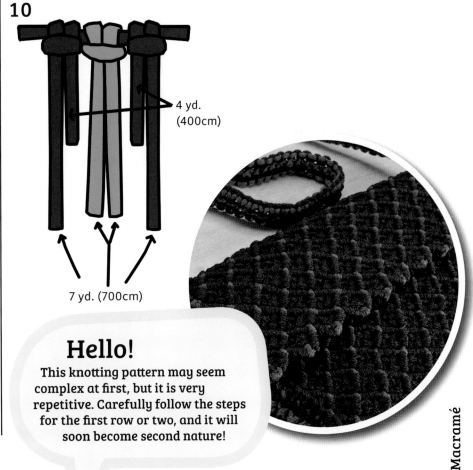

4 yd. (400cm)

7 yd. (700cm)

Hello!

This knotting pattern may seem complex at first, but it is very repetitive. Carefully follow the steps for the first row or two, and it will soon become second nature!

Macramé

Hello!

7| Starting at the left side, take the first three strands and use them to tie a square knot (figure 11). Repeat with the remaining strands across to form a row of square knots (figure 12). To keep a consistent color pattern, tie the square knots so the royal blue color always appears at the center of the knots, and the navy always appears at the outside edges.

8| Before starting the next row, cross the working strands between each square knot to stitch them together (figure 13). If the strands are not crossed, the knotting will continue in separate vertical rows. Cross the strands the same way throughout the design (e.g., always cross the right strand over the left) to keep the pattern consistent.

9| Continue the crossed square knot pattern until the strap/side piece is about 52" (132cm) long. To finish, weave the raw cord ends into the underside of the strap. Trim and melt any exposed ends to prevent fraying.

10| Fold the bottom edge of the bag up by 8"–10" (20.5–25.5cm), and position the ends of the strap/side piece in the bottom fold (figure 14). Using the extra cording from the guideline, sew the strap/side piece to the front and back of the bag. Sew the strap/side piece to the entire front of the bag, but only sew it 8"–10" (20.5–25.5cm) up the back of the bag (figure 15), leaving the remainder of the back free to form a flap. Trim and weave the cord ends into the inside of the bag. Melt any exposed ends to prevent fraying.

11| Cut the hook-and-loop tape into four 1½" (4cm) strips. Sew them to the front of the bag and the underside of the flap so they match up to form a closure.

11

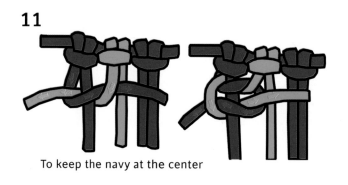

To keep the navy at the center

12

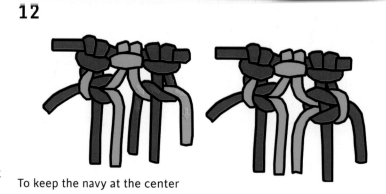

To keep the navy at the center

13

Cross the working strands between each knot (right over left)

14

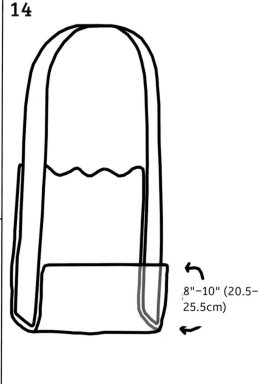

8"–10" (20.5–25.5cm)

15

Only sew 8"–10" (20.5–25.5cm) up the back

Hello!

16 **Macramé**

Simple Braided Rug »»»»» »»»»» »»»»»

FINISHED SIZE: 2' x 3' (70 x 91.5cm)

Put this rug anywhere—inside the front door or right in front of the kitchen sink. Customize the colors to match your décor!

TOOLS & MATERIALS

- 4mm craft cord:

  Four 16 yd. (16m) lengths in yellow

  Two 16 yd. (16m) lengths in orange

  Two 16 yd. (16m) lengths in bright pink

  Two 16 yd. (16m) lengths in neon green

  Two 16 yd. (16m) lengths in dark green

- Sewing needle

- Coordinating cotton or nylon thread

- Piece of foam core

- T-pins

- Scissors

- Grill lighter

1| Divide the 4mm cord colors into the following pairs: orange + yellow, yellow + neon green, orange + bright pink, dark green + neon green, yellow + bright pink, and yellow + dark green. Follow figures 1–4 to braid each color pair together in a four-strand flat braid. Finish each braid with a square knot (figures 5–6). When finished, you will have six braids.

2| Measure 3' (70cm) along one of the braids. At the 3' (70cm) mark, gently fold the braid back on itself, keeping it flat. Continue folding the braid in this manner every 3' (70cm) until you have a coil that is 3' (70cm) long and 4" (10cm) wide. It can be helpful to pin the braid to a piece of foam core during this step to keep it flat and hold the folds in place.

3| Once the coil is the proper shape and dimensions, sew it in place by stitching the rows of braid together along the long edges (figure 7).

4| Repeat steps 2–3 with the remaining braids. When finished, you will have six braided coils. Sew the coils together along the long edges to form the rug (figure 8).

5| If necessary, block the rug to adjust the shape. To do this, moisten the rug and pin it to a piece of foam core, adjusting the shape as desired. Dry under bright sunshine or direct heat. Note: Blocking can take several days.

1

2

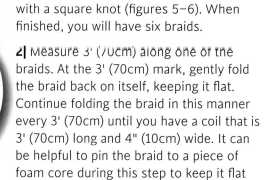

3

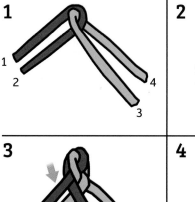

4

5

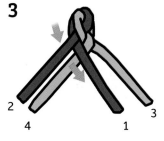

6

7

8

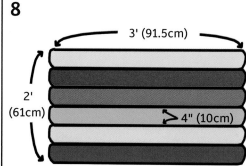

Patchwork Rug ››››››››››››››››››››››

FINISHED SIZE: 1½' x 2' (46 x 61cm)

This sturdy design makes a great welcome mat or bath mat!

TOOLS & MATERIALS

- 6mm craft cord in black, purple, light gray, and pale purple:

  Three 14 yd. (14m) lengths in each color

  Twenty-seven 1 yd. (100cm) lengths in each color

- 12 yd. (12m) of 2mm nylon cord in coordinating colors

- Sewing needle

- Splicing tool or large crochet hook

- Project board (or piece of foam core)

- T-pins

- Scissors

- Grill lighter

1| Each block requires one 14 yd. (14m) length and nine 1 yd. (100cm) lengths in the same color. To make a block, pin one end of a 14 yd. (14m) cord to the project board. Tie nine 1 yd. (100cm) strands in the same color onto the 14 yd. (14m) strand using lark's head knots. Position the attached strands so they span 6" (15cm) along the starting end of the 14 yd. (14m) strand.

2| Working from right to left, tie a half hitch knot around each of the attached strands with the 14 yd. (14m) strand. A quick way to do this is to form a "b" shape with the working strand and slip a vertical strand through the loop of the b from the back (figures 1–2). Tie half hitches across all the vertical strands with the 14 yd. (14m) strand (figure 3).

3| For the second row, turn and work from left to right to tie half hitches across the vertical cords. When working left to right, form a "d" shape with the working cord (figure 4), and slip each vertical strand through the loop from the back.

1

End of 14 yd. (14m) strand

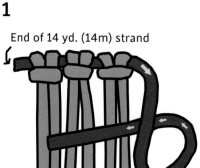

2

3

4

5

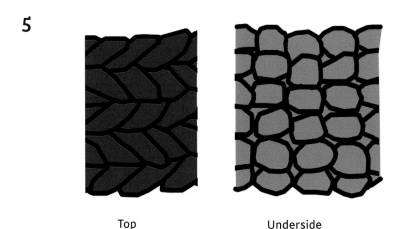

Top   Underside

6

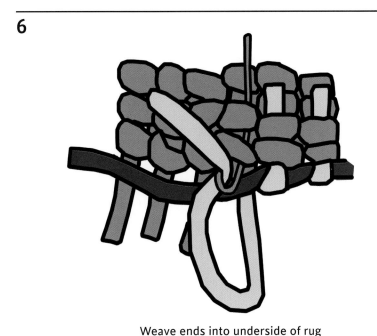

Weave ends into underside of rug

7

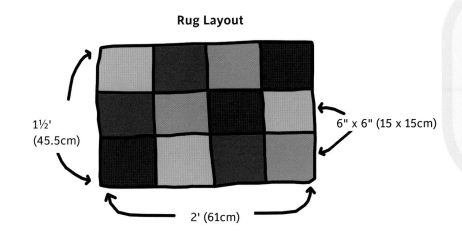

Rug Layout

1½' (45.5cm)

6" x 6" (15 x 15cm)

2' (61cm)

4| Continue creating rows of half hitches until the block is 6" (15cm) long. Remove the block from the project board and flip it over so you are looking at the underside (figure 5).

5| To finish the block, place the working strand against the bottom edge, over the vertical strands. Bring each vertical strand over the working strand, and use a splicing tool or crochet hook to weave them into the underside of the block (figure 6). After all vertical strands have been woven in, weave the end of the working strand into the underside of the block. Trim the cord ends and melt them to prevent fraying. You can hide the melted tips in the loops on the underside of the block.

6| Repeat steps 1–5 to create eleven additional blocks. Arrange the blocks in a pattern of your liking to form the rug, or see figure 7. Sew the edges of the blocks together with the nylon cord.

Hello!

The blocks for this rug have a pleasing knotted pattern on both the top and bottom, so you can position them as desired (with tops up or bottoms up). To add interesting texture, flip some blocks top side up, and some blocks bottom side up.

Macramé

Circle Swirls Rug >>>>>>>>>>>>>>>>>>

FINISHED SIZE: Approximately 4' x 3' (122 x 91.5cm)

Pump up the cute factor with this fun-filled design! Use it as a rug or a wall hanging.

TOOLS & MATERIALS

- 4mm craft cord in orange, yellow, neon green, dark green, bright pink, and blue:

  Two 7 yd. (700cm) lengths for each small circle

  Two 9 yd. (900cm) lengths for each medium circle

  Two 11 yd. (11m) lengths for each large circle

- Needle
- Coordinating thread
- Scissors
- Grill lighter

CIRCLE COLOR CHART

Circle Type	Colors
Large (6 circles)	Blue + Blue
	Pink + Pink
	Pink + Orange
	Orange + Yellow
	Yellow + Neon Green
	Neon Green + Dark Green
Medium (6 circles)	Orange + Orange
	Dark Green + Dark Green
	Neon Green + Neon Green
	Yellow + Yellow
	Yellow + Pink
	Blue + Neon Green
Small (12 circles)	Pink + Pink
	Green + Green
	Orange + Orange
	Blue + Blue
	Dark Green + Dark Green
	Yellow + Yellow
	Yellow + Pink
	Yellow + Orange
	Yellow + Neon Green
	Neon Green + Dark Green
	Neon Green + Blue
	Orange + Pink

1

1   2   3   4

2

1   2   3   4

1| Follow the circle color chart (right) to pair off the colors and lengths of the 4mm cord. Braid the color pairs for each circle together in a four-strand round braid. To form the braid, bring the outer right strand under the two in the center and back over one to the right. Bring the outer left strand under the two in the center and back over one to the left. Repeat this pattern, alternating left and right (figures 1–5). Finish each braid with a box stitch (figures 6–10).

Macramé

Hello!

The four-strand round braid can be a little tricky. If you're just learning it, start with the braids that require two different cord colors to get the rhythm of the braid pattern down. The different colors will help you see the pattern as you work. Then progress to braids that use two cords of the same color.

3

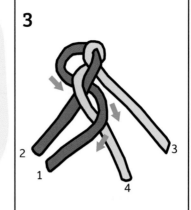

4

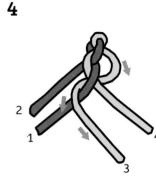

5

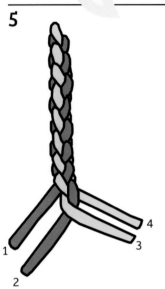

6

7

8

9

10

12

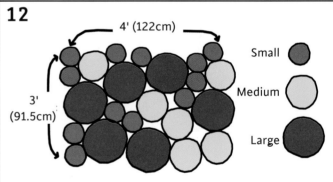

4' (122cm)

3'
(91.5cm)

Small

Medium

Large

2| Form each circle by coiling the braids around themselves to form flat disks. Sew the coils in place by stitching from the outside of each one toward the center, catching every row of the braid as you go (figure 11).

3| Arrange the circles in a pattern of your liking, or follow the pattern provided (figure 12). As you arrange the circles, make sure each one has at least two points of contact with the others. Sew the circles together where they touch.

11

Nautical Place Mat ›››› › ›››››› ›››

FINISHED SIZE: 12" x 18"
(30.5 x 45.5cm)

Give your kitchen the feel of the ocean with this marine-inspired place mat. One makes a great addition to a sea-themed centerpiece, or you can make a full set.

MATERIALS

- 75 yd. (75m) of 6mm craft cord, cut into 10–12 yd. (10–12m) lengths
- 20" x 15" (51 x 38cm) piece of foam core
- T-pins (about 25)
- Pen or pencil

- Ruler
- Splicing tool
- Sewing needle
- Coordinating thread
- Scissors
- Grill lighter

1

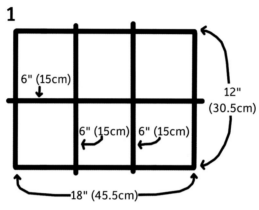

X = pins placed at 3" (7.5cm) intervals

3

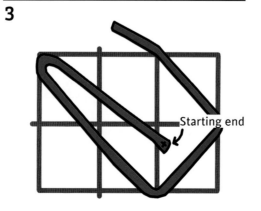

Starting end

1| Using a ruler and pencil, draw an 18" x 12" (45.5 x 30.5cm) rectangle on the foam core. On each side of the rectangle, measure and make a mark every 6" (15cm). You will make one mark on the short sides of the rectangle, and two marks on the long sides. Connect the marks with straight lines to form a grid with 6" (15cm) squares (figure 1).

2| Follow figure 2 to place T-pins along and within the grid. Note: Some T-pins are placed where the grid lines intersect; the others are placed 3" (7.5cm) along or away from a grid line.

3| Wrap a cord around the T-pins on the foam core, following figures 3–10 to form the first wrap of the nautical pattern. When you reach the starting point, use the working end to trace the first wrap all the way through the knot, always keeping the working end on the same side of the cord you are tracing (figure 10). Do not cross the working strand over any part of the cord you are tracing. Keep your wraps fairly loose as you work so you can weave the cord over and under strands as needed.

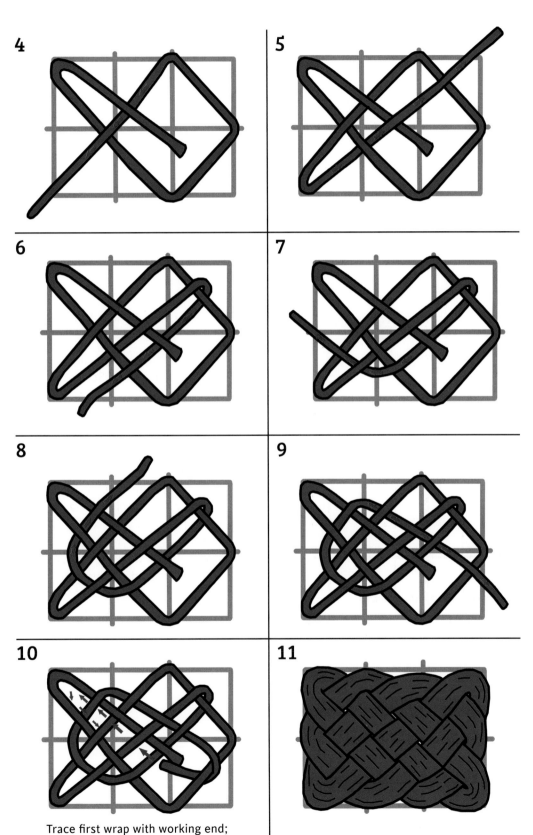

4 | Continue tracing the knot with the working end of the cord, keeping the wraps loose. When you begin to run out of cord, splice a new cord onto the working end (see page 6). Hide the spliced ends under the weaves of the knot pattern. Move or add T-pins as necessary to help maintain the shape of the knot as it grows.

5 | Continue tracing the knot until you have done 8–10 wraps. For a knot without spaces, continue making wraps until the knot is filled in to your liking (figure 11).

6 | To finish, sew the strands together to keep the knot from unraveling. Sew each strand to the strands next to it. Also sew the upper strands to the lower strands where the strands cross over each other in the weave. Remove the T-pins as you work each section. When finished, weave any loose cords into the underside of the mat and melt the ends.

Trace first wrap with working end; don't cross cords

Macramé

Hello!   27

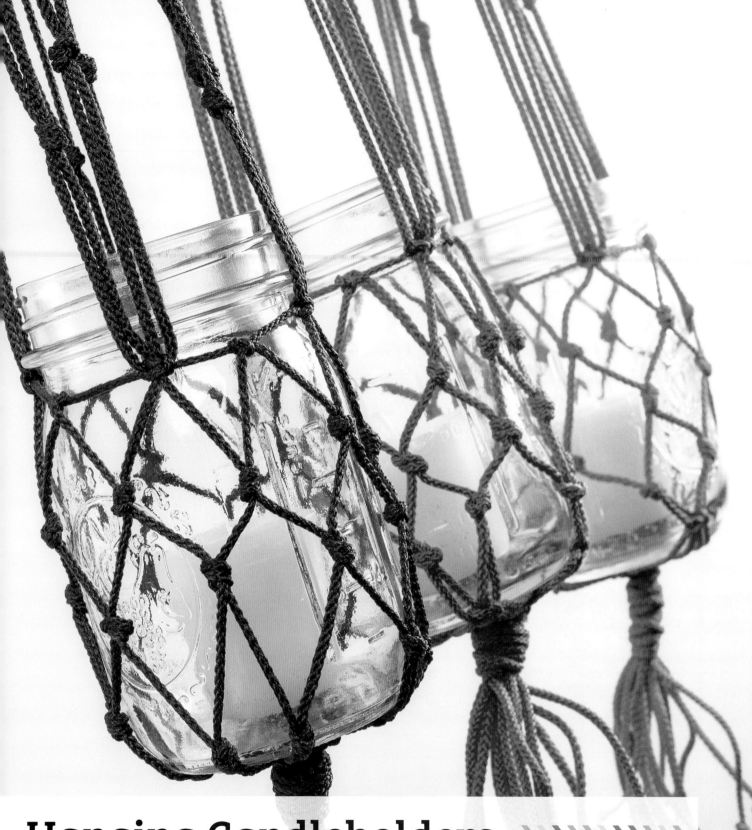

Hanging Candleholders >>>>>>>>>

FINISHED SIZE: 36" (91.5cm) long

These little hanging jars are perfect indoors and out!
Fill them with candles or use other decorative items like
shells, colored glass, or flowers.

TOOLS & MATERIALS

- 2mm craft cord
  - One 1 yd. (1m) length
  - Eight 3½ yd. (3.5m) lengths
- One 1" (2.5cm) ring
- 1 mason jar (no lid required)
- 1 floating candle kit or tea light candle with sand
- Grill lighter
- Scissors

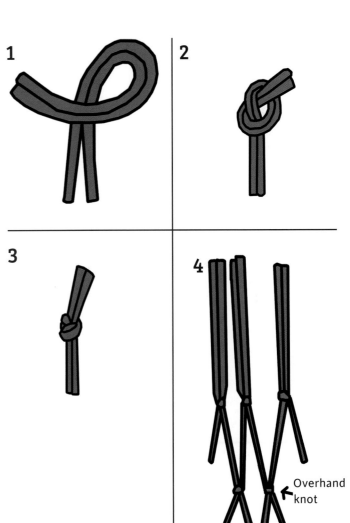

1| Thread and center eight 3½ yd. (350cm) cords on the ring. Tie each cord onto the ring using a single strand overhand knot.

2| Position the cords so there are eight at the front of the ring and eight at the back of the ring. Tie the front cords together in pairs, about 6"–8" (15–20.5cm) from the ring, using overhand knots. Repeat with the back cords (figures 1–3).

3| Take two adjacent overhand knots. Use one strand from the left knot and one strand from the right knot to tie an overhand knot 6"–8" (15–20.5cm) from the previous knots. Repeat with all the remaining strands until the second row is complete (figure 4).

4| Repeat step 3, alternating the knots on each row to form a loose, tubular net. Continue knotting this way until the net is about 24" (61cm) long.

5| Using four adjacent strands, tie a square knot (see page 4) 6"–8" (15–20.5cm) from the previous row of knots. Repeat with the remaining strands, making sure all the square knots are level with one another.

Overhand knot

5

6

7

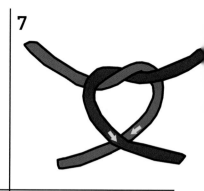

8

9

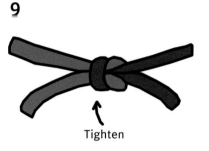

Tighten

10

Hello!

These hanging jars are also perfect for holding home décor items. Try filling them with seashells, glass marbles, or other collectibles you might want to display.

6| Place the four square knots around the top of the mason jar. To tighten the cords around the top of the jar, take two adjacent square knots. Use the right working strand from the left knot and the left working strand from the right knot to tie a reef knot (figures 5–9). Repeat with the remaining working strands (figure 10). Be sure these knots are tight around the jar opening. The jar should not be loose.

7| Form a net around the body of the jar using a series of alternating overhand knots as you did to form the net above the jar. The knots should be spaced no more than 2" (5cm) apart. Knot to the underside of the jar.

8| Hold the cords together at the bottom of the jar, in the center. Wrap the cords together (see page 7) using the 1 yd. (100cm) cord so they remain in place at the bottom center of the jar.

9| Trim the cord ends even with one another, and melt the tips to prevent fraying. For a more decorative touch, tie the end of each cord in an overhand knot. Place floating candles or tea lights in the jar.

Retro Plant Hangers >>>>>>>>>>>>>

Update these 1970s favorites with modern colors and designs. Use them to hold glass bowls filled with décor items, or stick with the traditional plants.

Striped Twist >>>>>>>>>>>>

FINISHED SIZE: 36" (91.5cm) long (small),
48" (122cm) long (large)

TOOLS & MATERIALS

- 4mm craft cord;

  Four 5 yd. (500cm) lengths
  in color A (6.5 yd. [650cm]
  for large size)

  Four 5 yd. (500cm) lengths
  in color B (6.5 yd. [650cm]
  for large size)

  Four 3.5 yd. (350cm) lengths
  in color B (4 yd. [400cm] for
  large size)

  One 1 yd. (100cm) length in
  color B (both sizes)

- Scissors

- Grill lighter

- One 2" (5cm) metal ring

- One 32mm wooden bead with
  large opening

1| Find the center points of the 3.5 yd. (350cm) strands, and tie them onto the metal ring using lark's head knots.

2| Thread the wooden bead onto all of the cords attached to the ring, positioning the bead against the ring.

3| Center a 5 yd. (500cm) strand in color A behind two strands attached to the ring and tie a half knot with it (figures 1–2). Repeat with a 5 yd. (500cm) strand in color B to tie a second half knot directly below the first (figure 3).

1

2

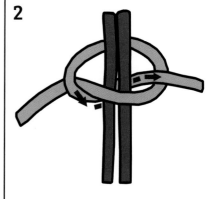

3

4

5

6

7

4" (10cm)

Square knot with four center strands

8

3" (7.5cm)

2" (5cm)

4| Carry the working strands from the first knot and bring one in front of and one behind the second knot. Tie a half knot with the working strands (figure 4). Continue in this manner, tying half knots around the center strands, alternating colors, to form a spiral pattern (figures 5–6).

5| Continue knotting until the spiral is 20"–22" (51–56cm) long (26"–28" [66–71cm] long for large size). Repeat steps 3–4 three times to form the other three spirals. Check the spiral lengths as you work to make sure they are even. When finished, you will have four long spirals attached to the ring.

6| Take two adjacent spirals and measure down 4" (10cm) from the ends. Use three strands from the left spiral and three strands from the right spiral to tie a square knot. Form the knot with two working strands and four center strands (figure 7). Repeat with the remaining strands extending from the spirals.

7| For the next row, take two adjacent square knots, measure down 3" (7.5cm), and use three strands from the left square knot and three strands from the right square knot to tie a square knot. Repeat with the remaining strands.

8| Repeat step 7 to tie a final row of square knots. This time, measure down 2" (5cm) from the previous row (figure 8).

9| Grasp the loose cord ends just below the last row of knots. Using the 1 yd. (100cm) strand, wrap the cords together (see page 7) as close to the bottom row of square knots as possible, making sure the wrap is centered. Trim the cords to the desired length. Melt or knot the ends to prevent fraying.

Macramé

Hello! 33

Two-Tone Braid >>>>>>>>

FINISHED SIZE: 4½' (137cm) long

TOOLS & MATERIALS

- 6mm craft cord:
    - Four 5 yd. (500cm) lengths in color A
    - Four 5 yd. (500cm) lengths in color B
    - One 1 yd. (100cm) length in either color
- Scissors
- Grill lighter
- One 2" (5cm) metal ring
- Eight 20mm wooden beads with large openings

1

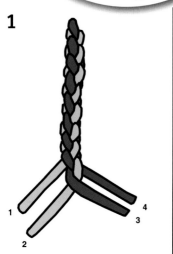

2

3

4

Tighten

1| Thread and center two 5 yd. (500cm) cords, one in color A and one in color B, on the ring. Follow figures 1–5 of the Circle Swirls Rug (page 22) to braid the strands together in a four-strand round braid (figure 1). Continue until the braid is about 1 yd. (100cm) long. Finish the braid with a square knot (figures 2–4).

2| Thread a bead onto the two center strands of the square knot, positioning it against the square knot. Secure the bead in place by tying a square knot below it (figure 5).

3| Repeat steps 1–2 with the remaining 5 yd. (500cm) strands. Check the braid lengths as you work to make sure they are even. When finished, you will have four long braids attached to the ring.

4| Take two adjacent braids and measure down 4" (10cm) from the ends. Use two strands from the left braid and two strands from the right braid to tie a square knot. Thread a bead onto the center strands, and tie a square knot below it (figure 6).

5

Add bead and tie a second square knot

6

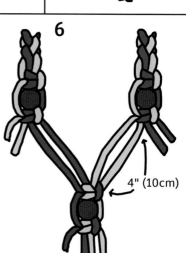

4" (10cm)

5| Follow the process from steps 7 and 8 for the Striped Twist plant hanger (page 32) to form the next two rows of square knots. Use four strands for each square knot instead of six. Add beads if desired.

6| Follow step 9 for the Striped Twist plant hanger (page 32) to wrap and finish the cord ends.

Hello!

Triple Basket Hanger ⟩⟩⟩⟩⟩⟩⟩⟩

FINISHED SIZE: 4' (122cm) long

TOOLS & MATERIALS

- 2mm nylon cord:

  Twelve 6 yd. (600cm) lengths

  Three 1 yd. (100cm) lengths

- Scissors

- Grill lighter

- Rubber bands (optional)

- One 1½" (4cm) metal ring

1| Find the center points of the 6 yd. (600cm) strands and tie them onto the metal ring using lark's head knots.

2| Divide the cords into six groups of four cords each. Take one group and tie alternating half hitches with the cords (figures 1–2). Try to keep the cords parallel as you work to produce a wavy pattern (figure 3). Knot for 12" (30.5cm), and then finish with a square knot (figures 4–5).

3| Repeat step 2 with the remaining groups of cords. Check the knotted cord lengths as you work to make sure they are even. When finished, you will have six knotted cords attached to the ring.

4| Take two adjacent knotted cords and measure down 3" (7.5cm) from the ends. Use two strands from the left knotted cord and two strands from the right knotted cord to tie a square knot (figure 6). Repeat with the remaining strands extending from the knotted cords.

Hello!

This is the ultimate plant hanger—it can hold up to three 6" (5cm) wide pots!

1
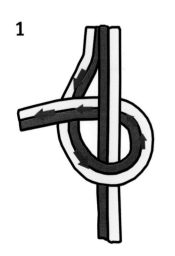

2
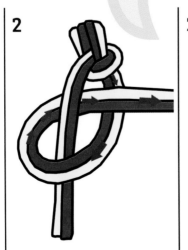

3

4

5

Macramé

Hello! 35

5| For the next row, take two adjacent square knots, measure down 1½" (4cm), and use two strands from the left square knot and two strands from the right square knot to tie a square knot. Repeat with the remaining strands.

6| Repeat step 5 to tie a final row of square knots. This time, measure down ½" (1.5cm) from the previous row.

7| Measure down 6" (15cm) from the last row of square knots. For a consistent pattern, use rubber bands or form infinity bundles (page 5) to secure each group of four strands together so you can identify them later. Then gather all the cords together below the final row of knots. Using one of the 1 yd. (100cm) cords, tie a series of half knots around the cords (figures 7–8). The half knot wrap should be about 2"–3" (5–7.5cm) long and will spiral around the cords (figure 9).

8| Unfurl the infinity bundles you made in step 7 and work with each cord group one at a time for the following steps. Repeat steps 2–7 twice to form two additional baskets. After tying the final half knot wrap, trim the cords to the desired length. Knot or melt the ends to prevent fraying. When finished, you will have a plant hanger with three baskets (figure 10).

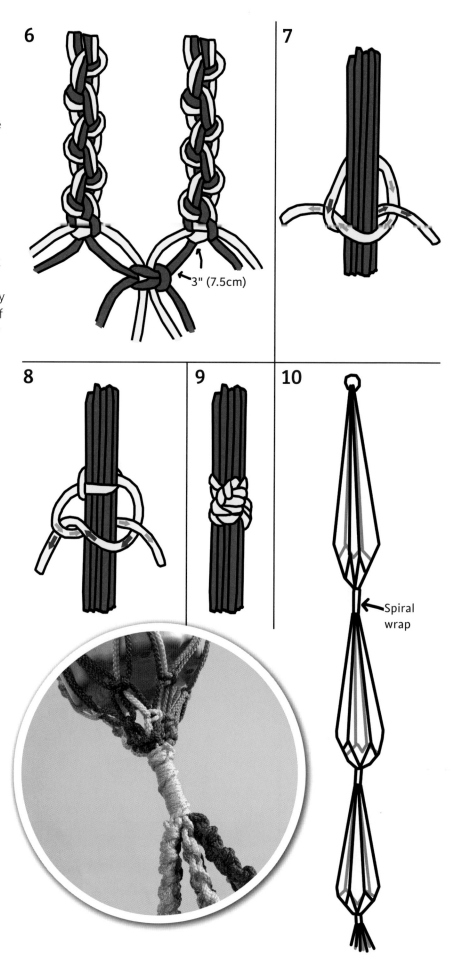

6

3" (7.5cm)

7

8

9

10

Spiral wrap

Covered Cushion >>>>>>>>>>>>>>>>

FINISHED SIZE: About 20" (51cm) in diameter

Use this design to make floor pillows for casual seating, or even accent pillows for your outdoor furniture.

Hello!
For this project, it is best to work on a large flat surface, such as a table, to keep the circles flat.

TOOLS & MATERIALS

- 6mm craft cord:

  Two 35 yd. (35m) lengths

  Twenty 6 yd. (600cm) lengths

  Eleven 5 yd. (500cm) lengths (set one aside for step 15)

  Ten 2½ yd. (250cm) lengths

- Several 6" (15cm) scraps of string in contrasting color

- 18"–20" (45.5 x 51cm) diameter round pillow, 4" (10cm) thick, or a 27' x 12" (823 x 61cm) roll of 1" (2.5cm) foam

- 2 yd. (200cm) of nylon or vinyl fabric (can cover up to two pillows)

- Splicing tool or crochet hook

- Sewing needle or sewing machine

- Coordinating thread

- Scissors

- Grill lighter

1| Form a 1½" (4cm) ring with one end of a 35 yd. (35m) strand (figure 1). Secure the ring in place by tying five of the 6 yd. (600cm) strands around it using lark's head knots. Be sure to tie a knot over the place where the strands forming the ring cross (figures 2–3). Tighten the ring by tugging gently on the long strand forming it. This is the guideline.

2| Using a lark's head knot, tie a scrap of string onto the guideline where it exits the ring to mark your starting point (figure 4).

3| Working counter clockwise, bring the guideline around the initial ring and tie every strand extending from the ring onto it using a double half hitch (figure 5). Continue working around the initial ring until you reach the starting point marked by the scrap of string. This completes round 1.

4| For rounds 2 and 3, repeat step 3.

5| On round 4, you will attach five 6 yd. (600cm) strands to the guideline using lark's head knots. Continue to tie strands already attached to the initial ring onto the guideline using double half hitches. Complete round 4 using the following pattern (the knots are now abbreviated DHH for double half hitch and LHK for lark's head knot): one DHH, one LHK, [two DHH, one LHK] four times, one DHH (figure 6).

1

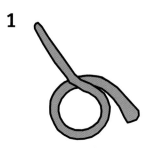

2

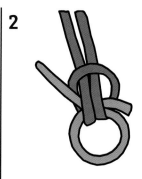

3

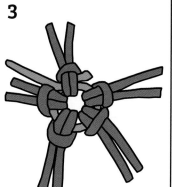

4

Place marker

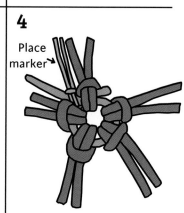

Hello!

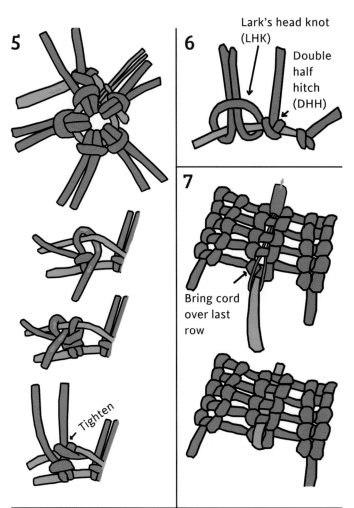

5

6
Lark's head knot (LHK)
Double half hitch (DHH)

7
Bring cord over last row

Tighten

6| For rounds 5–7, repeat step 3.

7| For round 8, add five 5 yd. (500cm) strands to the guideline using the following pattern: two DHH, one LHK, [four DHH, one LHK] four times, two DHH.

8| For rounds 9–13, repeat step 3.

9| For round 14, add five 2½ yd. (250cm) strands to the guideline using the following pattern: three DHH, one LHK, [six DHH, one LHK] four times, three DHH.

10| For rounds 15–19, repeat step 3.

11| Trim all the cord ends, including the guideline, so they are no longer than 10" (25.5cm). Flip the circle over and weave all the cord ends into the underside using a splicing tool or crochet hook (figure 7). Trim and melt the ends to prevent fraying.

12| Repeat steps 1–11 to form a second knotted circle.

13| Trace one of the knotted circles onto the fabric twice. Cut out the circles, cutting along the outside of your tracing lines. Trace one of the knotted circles onto the foam four times. Cut out the circles, cutting along the inside of your tracing lines. If you have a round pillow, skip tracing and cutting the foam circles. Cut one 4½" x 72" (11.5 x 183cm) piece of fabric. Mark ¼" (0.5cm) seam allowances on all pieces of fabric (figure 8).

14| Sew the fabric pieces together by stitching each long edge of the rectangle to one of the fabric circles. Leave a large opening in the seam to insert the foam or pillow. Stack the foam circles on top of one another. Roll up the foam stack or pillow and insert it into the fabric case. Sew the ends of the rectangle piece together, and sew the opening in the seam closed from the outside (figure 9).

15| Take the knotted circles and place one on the top and one on the bottom of the foam pillow. Tie the remaining 5 yd. (500cm) strand onto the outer edge of the top circle with a double half hitch. Bring the strand down to the outer edge of the bottom circle and wrap it around. Continue in this manner, zigzagging between the outer edges of the two circles to close the sides of the cushion (figure 10). Tighten and tie off any excess cords. Weave the cords back into the cushion and melt the ends to prevent fraying.

8

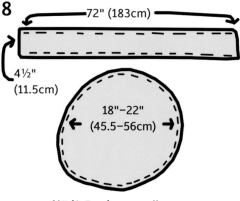

72" (183cm)

4½" (11.5cm)

18"–22" (45.5–56cm)

¼" (0.5cm) seam allowance

9

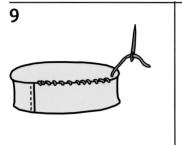

10

Macramé

Hello!

Hanging Chair

FINISHED SIZE: 4' (122cm) seat, 5' (152.5cm) long when suspended from ceiling

Hang this chair up inside or outside for a truly unique piece of furniture for you and your guests. Note: For extra safety, the support cords are made using eight strands instead of four. Alternatively, use 550 paracord to form the support cords using four strands instead of eight.

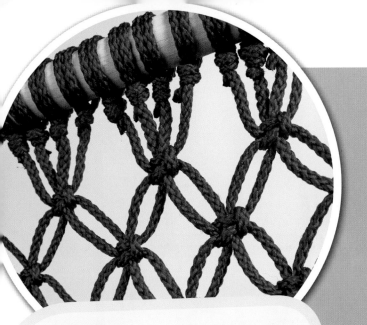

TOOLS & MATERIALS

- 6mm craft cord:

    Forty 5 yd. (500cm) lengths for the seat

    Eight 6 yd. (600cm) lengths for the front support

    Eight 4 yd. (400cm) lengths for the back support.

- 4 dowel caps

- Paintbrush

- All-weather outdoor primer/sealer

- Yardstick or ruler

- Scissors

- Grill lighter

- Splicing tool

- Two 3' (91.5cm) dowel rods, 2" (5cm) thick or thicker

- 4 industrial weight-bearing steel rings or links

- 4 mounting hooks or brackets (carabiners recommended)

Hello!

Your local home improvement store will be your best resource for sourcing the industrial-strength items and large dowels required for this project and the hammock.

1| Prime and seal the dowel rods if you plan to hang your chair outside, even if it will be on a covered porch. Attach the dowel caps to each end of both dowels to prevent the cords from sliding off as you work.

2| Thread a ring onto four 3 yd. (300cm) cords, placing the ring at the center point of the cords. Pair off the strands so you have four groups of two strands each and follow figures 1–5 of the Circle Swirls Rug (page 22) to braid the groups together in a four-strand round braid. Continue until the braid is about 1 yd. (100cm) long. Follow figures 6–10 of the Circle Swirls Rug (page 22) to finish the braid with a box stitch. This is one of the back supports.

3| Using the same ring from step 2, repeat step 2 with four 5 yd. (500cm) strands to attach a second braid to the ring. Make this braid 2 yd. (200cm) long. This is one of the front supports. When finished, you will have two braids attached to the ring: one 1 yd. (100cm) back support and one 2 yd. (200cm) front support.

4| Repeat steps 2–3 with one ring, four 3 yd. (300cm) strands, and four 5 yd. (500cm) strands to create the second front and back supports. Thread a ring onto each of the front supports.

5| Mount a 1 yd. (100cm) back support to each end of a dowel rod following the crown knot mounting illustrations (page 43). Form at least five to six crown knots to prevent the cords from unraveling. Adjust the crown knots as needed to make sure the back supports are even and the dowel rod will be level when the chair is hung up. After ensuring the dowel rod will be level, weave the loose cords into the braid. Trim the cords and melt the ends.

6| Mount the forty 5 yd. (500cm) strands onto the dowel rod with the back supports attached using the hitch and coil illustrations (page 44). Space the strands out evenly between the two back supports.

7| Create the seat for the chair using an alternating square knot pattern (see the alternate square knot illustrations on page 44). Starting on the left side, take the first four strands and use them to tie a square knot. Repeat across the remaining strands. For the next row, skip the first two strands, and begin tying square knots across the row as before. Skip the last two strands. Continue in this manner, alternating between full rows of square knots and rows of alternate square knots. Use a yardstick or ruler as a guide to keep the spacing between each row consistent.

8| Continue the alternating square knot pattern until the seat of the chair is about 4' (122cm) long. Then tie the cords onto the second dowel rod, following the hitch and coil illustrations (page 44).

9| Mount a 2 yd. (200cm) front support on each end of the second dowel rod following the crown knot mounting illustrations (page 43). Adjust the crown knots as needed to make sure the front supports are even and the dowel rod will be level when the chair is hung up. After ensuring the dowel rod will be level, trim the cords and melt the ends.

10| Use the mounting hooks or brackets to attach the chair to a ceiling, positioning the rings attached to the front supports about 1' (30.5cm) away from each other (see the chair mounting illustration at the right).

Chair Mounting

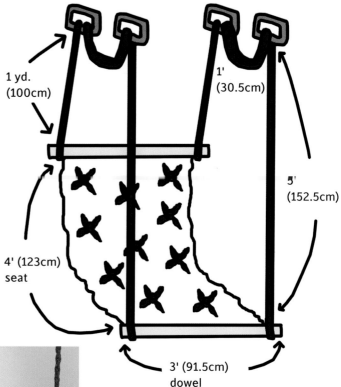

1 yd. (100cm)

1' (30.5cm)

5' (152.5cm)

4' (123cm) seat

3' (91.5cm) dowel

Hello!

Crown Knot Mounting Illustrations

1

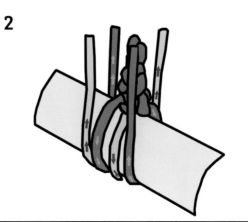

2

3

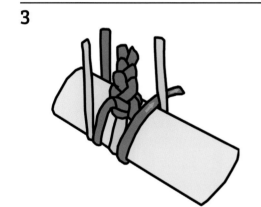

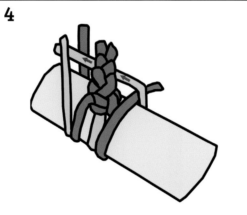

4

5

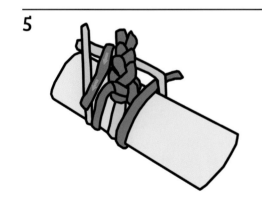

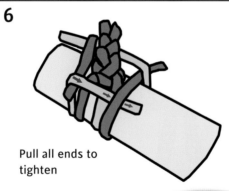

6

Pull all ends to tighten

7

Weave loose cords into braid

Hitch and Coil Illustrations

Alternate Square Knot Illustrations

1

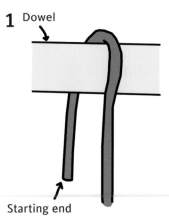

Dowel

Starting end

2

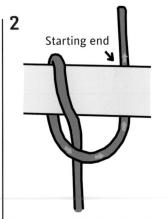

Starting end

1

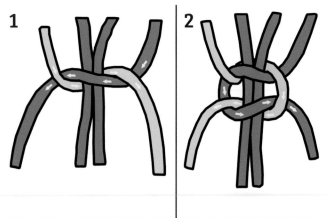

2

3

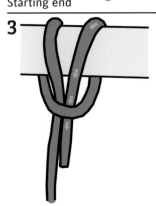

Tighten against dowel

4

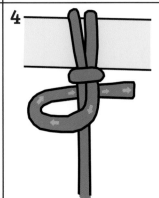

3

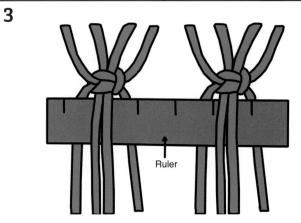

Ruler

5

Wrap two to three times with starting end

6

Pass starting end through center of coil

4

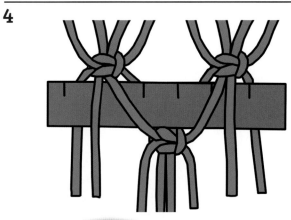

7

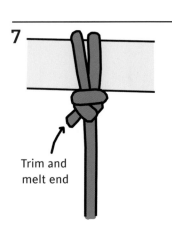

Trim and melt end

Hammock

>>>>>>>>>>>>>>>>>>>>>>>>>>>>>

FINISHED SIZE: Finished size: 9' (274.5cm) long

This project is for advanced and patient crafters, but once you're finished, it will give you a comfy spot to relax and dream up your next macramé project!

TOOLS & MATERIALS

- 6mm craft cord:

    Twenty 3 yd. (300cm) lengths

    Twenty-four 4 yd. (400cm) lengths

    Sixty 7 yd. (700cm) lengths

- 4 dowel caps
- Paintbrush
- All-weather outdoor primer/sealer
- Yardstick or ruler
- Scissors
- Grill lighter

- Splicing tool
- Two 4' (122cm) dowel rods, 2" (5cm) thick or thicker
- 2 industrial weight-bearing steel rings or links
- 2 mounting hooks or brackets (carabiners recommended)
- 2 industrial eye hooks (only necessary for hammock made without cord ends, see eye hook mounting illustration below)

1| Prime and seal the dowel rods if you plan to hang your hammock outside, even if it will be on a covered porch. Attach the dowel caps to each end of both dowels to prevent the cords from sliding off as you work.

2| For a hammock without the cord ends, find the center point on the length of the two dowels and install an eye hook on each dowel at this point following the manufacturer's instructions (see the eye hook mounting illustration below). Skip to step 6.

3| For a hammock with cord ends, you will attach eleven braids to each ring for each cord end. To do this, thread a ring onto two 4 yd. (400cm) cords, placing the ring at the center point of the cords. Follow figures 1–5 of the Circle Swirls Rug (page 22) to braid the strands together in a four-strand round braid. Follow figures 6–10 of the Circle Swirls Rug (page 22) to finish the braid with a box stitch. Using the same ring, repeat to attach two more braids using 4 yd. (400cm) cords, then five braids using 3 yd. (300cm) cords, then three braids using 4 yd. (400cm) cords. You will need to adjust the braid lengths so the cord end forms a triangle when attached to

Cord End

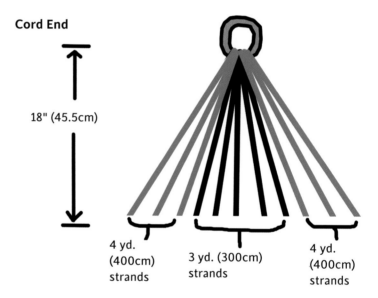

18" (45.5cm)

4 yd. (400cm) strands

3 yd. (300cm) strands

4 yd. (400cm) strands

Eye Hook Mounting

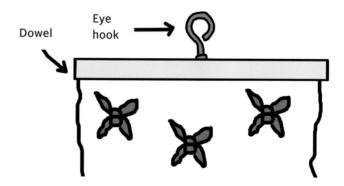

Dowel

Eye hook

the dowel rod and holds the dowel level. This means the braids at the outer edges need to be longer than those at the center. Line the ends of the braids up against one of the dowels as you work to help determine the lengths. Here are some approximate measurements, working from left to right: 28" (71cm), 24" (61cm), 21" (53.5cm), 19" (48cm), 17" (43cm), 17" (43cm), 17" (43cm), 19" (48cm), 21" (53.5cm), 24" (61cm), 28" (71cm).

4| Repeat step 3 with the remaining ring and the remaining 3 yd. (300cm) and 4 yd. (400cm) cords to form the other cord end.

5| Take one of the cord ends and, working from the outer braids toward the center braids, mount the braids onto one of the dowels, following the crown knot mounting illustrations (page 43). Adjust the crown knots as needed to make sure the braids will hold the dowel rod level when the hammock is hung up. After ensuring the dowel rod will be level, trim the cords and melt the ends. Repeat with the second cord end and dowel rod.

6| Take one of the dowel rods and mount all of the 7 yd. (700cm) cords onto it following the hitch and coil illustrations (page 44). Space the strands out evenly along the length of the dowel between the attached braids.

7| Repeat step 7 from the Hanging Chair (page 40) to tie the bed of the hammock using an alternate square knot pattern. Continue until the bed of the hammock is about 6'-7' (183–213.5cm) long or the length you desire. Then tie the cords onto the second dowel rod following the hitch and coil illustrations (page 44). See the hammock layout illustration to check your progress.

8| Use the mounting hooks or brackets to hang the hammock in a relaxing spot!

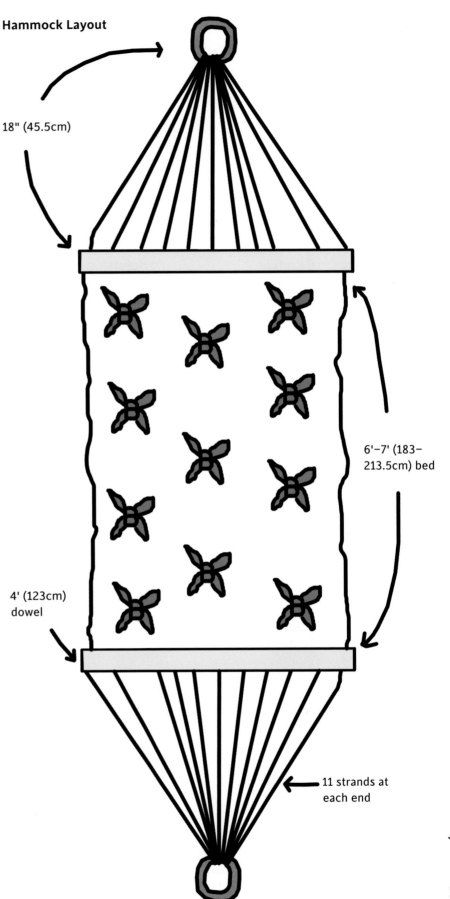

Hammock Layout

18" (45.5cm)

6'-7' (183–213.5cm) bed

4' (123cm) dowel

11 strands at each end

Macramé

Hello!   47

More Great Books from Design Originals

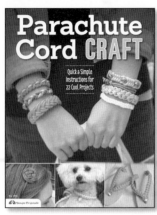

Parachute Cord Craft
ISBN 978-1-57421-371-3 **$9.99**
DO3495

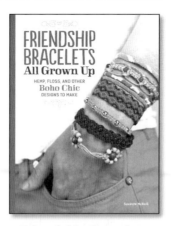

Friendship Bracelets
ISBN 978-1-57421-866-4 **$9.99**
DO5440

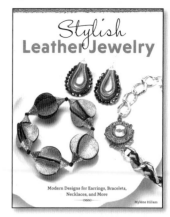

Stylish Leather Jewelry
ISBN 978-1-57421-401-7 **$16.99**
DO5372

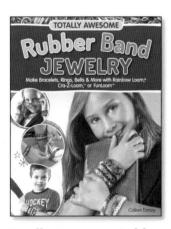

**Totally Awesome Rubber
Band Jewelry**
ISBN 978-1-57421-896-1 **$7.99**
DO5454

Epic Rubber Band Crafts
ISBN 978-1-57421-914-2 **$7.99**
DO5472

**Hooked on Rubber
Band Jewelry**
ISBN 978-1-57421-915-9 **$7.99**
DO5473

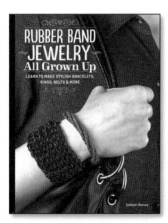

**Rubber Band Jewelry
All Grown Up**
ISBN 978-1-57421-916-6 **$9.99**
DO5474

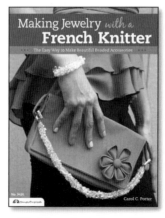

**Making Jewelry with
a French Knitter**
ISBN 978-1-57421-363-8 **$8.99**
DO3486

Bead Weaving on a Loom
ISBN 978-1-57421-384-3 **$8.99**
DO3507